Who is Muhammad Ali? Why is he famous? Why did he have two names, Cassius Clay in his early years, and later Muhammad Ali? And what is he doing now?

Muhammad Ali was, of course, a famous boxer, a world champion. But he fought for black Americans, too. He stopped boxing in 1981 because he was sick. But today he is fighting for peace in the world.

The Red and White Bike

The story starts with a boy's new red and white bike.

It is 1954. Joe Martin is a policeman in Louisville Kentucky, but he teaches boxing in a gym in the evenings, too.

One day two young black boys come into the gym. One of them sees Joe.

"Excuse me," he says. "Are you Joe Martin, the policeman?"

"That's right," Joe says. "What's your problem?"

"It's my new bike," the boy says. "It's red and white. It was in front of this building, and now it's not there."

The young boy is unhappy and very angry.

"I'm going to find the boy with my bike. Then I'm going to *whup** him!" he says again and again.

Joe Martin smiles. The boy is about twelve years old. He is tall with long legs, and he is thin.

"Can you box?" Joe asks.

"No, I can't box," the boy says. "But I want to whup that boy."

*whup: to fight and beat a person (Black A⌐

1

Cassius Clay at twelve years old

Joe smiles again. "Come here to the gym first. Maybe I can teach you."

"OK," the boy says. "I'd like that."

"Good," Joe says. "What's your name?"

"Cassius," the boy says. "Cassius Clay."

Joe doesn't know it, but in only ten years that young black boy is going to be a world boxing champion!

After that, Cassius went to Joe Martin's gym six days a week. He was strong and quick on his feet, and he started boxing with the other boys in the gym. He didn't box for money, of course. He boxed because he liked it. He usually won his fights. He was good!

But he wasn't a good student at school. He had a lot of problems. He was a good boy from a good family. He was friendly and his teachers liked him. But school work was very difficult for him. The only important thing in the world for him then was boxing.

In six years he had 108 fights and he won 100 of them.

Then in 1960 he went to Rome and boxed for the United States.

The Olympic Games

In 1960 Cassius was only eighteen years old. He was in Rome for the Olympic Games.* He beat every opponent and he won an Olympic medal for the United States. He was an Olympic boxing champion. And he didn't take off his Olympic medal for weeks—night or day.

*Olympic Games: people from every country go to these Games every four years and some win medals

Eighteen-year-old Cassius Clay was an Olympic champion.

At home in Louisville he was famous. But he was black. And in Louisville in the 1960s there were places for white people and places for black people.

In many hotels, theaters, stores, and buses, black people didn't sit with white people. One day Cassius wanted to buy a drink in a "white" store. It was a problem. "Whites only," they said.

"But I'm the Olympic boxing champion—I'm famous," Cassius said.

"Whites only," they answered. "Go away!"

Cassius was very unhappy about that. "I'm going to be the World Champion," he said. "I'm going to be important. Then white people are going to sit down with me and listen to me."

After the Olympic Games Cassius started to fight for money. Boxing wasn't a game now. It was his work. He moved from Louisville to Miami. He went to a new gym in Miami, and he had new friends. One of them was

Angelo Dundee. He worked with Cassius in the gym and was always with him for his fights.

The First Fight with Sonny Liston

In 1964 Cassius Clay was twenty-two years old. He was tall and strong. After nineteen fights and nineteen wins, he wanted to fight the world champion, Sonny Liston.

Clay always moved very quickly in his fights. He danced here and there in the ring. His opponents were big, strong men. But they lost because their punches usually didn't hit him.

But Liston was the world champion and a very strong boxer. The newspapers in the U.S. said, "Liston is going to win this fight. Clay is very young. Liston is going to kill him." Only three newspapers said, "Maybe Clay can beat the champion."

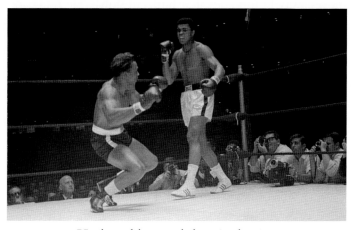

He danced here and there in the ring.

The fight was in Miami, and it was on television in a lot of American theaters, too.

Young Cassius Clay wanted to be famous and make a lot of money. Before his fights he played a game. He talked and talked. Usually boxers were quiet men, but Clay's mouth was always open.

Before every fight he said to the people and the newspapers, "I'm beautiful. I'm good. I'm quick and strong. I'm going to beat that man in two, or three, or four rounds." White people were angry with him. They didn't like this young black man with the big mouth. "Kill him!" they said to his opponents. "Close that big mouth for him." But then, of course, a lot of people wanted to see the fight.

Before the fight with Sonny Liston, Clay played this same game. Liston was very strong, but he wasn't very quick.

The fight is on February 25. In round 1 Clay starts to dance. Liston can't hit him. Sometimes Clay hits his opponent's face—one, two very quick punches. Then he moves away. Liston goes after him, but slowly. He is big and strong, but he can't hit the young Clay.

Clay goes back to his chair. He smiles at his friend, Angelo Dundee. "That's the first round, and he didn't kill me," he says. "I can win this." Liston is on his feet. He doesn't want to sit down. He wants to start round 2.

But it is the same story in rounds 2 and 3 and 4. Clay dances across the ring and Liston can't catch him. Sometimes he hits Clay, of course, but Clay is always moving away. And he is hitting Liston's face and eyes all the time.

After six rounds, Liston sits down. His face is red and one eye is closing. Suddenly he is very tired. "That man can hit!" he says.

Now it is round 7 and Clay is standing up on his feet. He is waiting, but his opponent isn't moving from his chair. Cassius Clay is the new champion of the world and he is only twenty-two years old.

He calls to the newspaper men near the ring. "I am the champion. I'm beautiful. I'm number one in the world. And you were all wrong, wrong, wrong!"

"And you were all wrong, wrong, wrong."

A New Name and New Problems

The day after that first fight with Liston, Cassius Clay had a new name. "My name is not Cassius Clay now," he said. "It's Muhammad Ali."

Ali's family was unhappy about this. His father, "Cash" Clay, and his mother were good Christian people. Their two sons were always good Christians, too. They loved their mother and father and had a happy home.

"What's wrong with the name 'Clay'?" his father asked. "It's a good name. It's our name."

"Clay is a white man's name," Ali said. "We have that name because our family worked for Mr. Clay, a white man. Our family came from Africa, and I would like a new name, a 'black' name. And from today, I'm going to be a Muslim, because in the U.S. *white* people are Christians. My black brothers are Muslims and I'm going to be a Muslim, too."

Later that year Ali visited Egypt and Africa. He talked to Muslims there. "There are Muslims of all colors in the world," he said. "I know that now. Our problem in the U.S. is only with the bad white people there." But he liked his new Muslim name and he stayed a Muslim.

Fifteen months later he and Sonny Liston fought again. This time Liston was on his face on the floor in the first round. Muhammad Ali was the world boxing champion.

In 1967 the U.S. Army was in Vietnam. Thousands of young Americans, white and black, went into the U.S. Army and fought the Vietcong. The U.S. government called Muhammad Ali and said, "Your country wants you in the army. You have to go to Vietnam."

Ali answered, "I'm a Muslim and Muslims want peace. They don't fight and kill people. Who are the Vietcong? They don't want to kill me, and I don't want to kill them. I'm not going to go into the army!"

This was a big problem. The U.S. government said, "Go into the army, or go to jail." The American people were angry with Ali, and they really didn't

"Go into the army, or go to jail."

like him. "You can't box in the U.S. You can't be world champion," the government said. "And you can't go and box in other countries." But Ali didn't go into the army.

"I'm a boxer," he said. "I fight people because that's my job. But I don't kill people."

Ali didn't box for two years. He talked to students in schools and got a little money. He talked about peace in Vietnam. "The fighting in Vietnam is wrong," he always said.

The government didn't send him to jail, but he didn't have much money. Then in 1970 the U.S. government said, "You can box again."

But there was a new world champion now, Joe Frazier.

Joe Frazier, A New Opponent

Joe Frazier was a good boxer. He was strong and quick. He was an Olympic champion, too. He won his medal at the Olympic Games in Tokyo in 1964. Ali's first fight with him was in New York in 1971.

But two years away from boxing is a long time. The fight was very difficult for Ali. He danced, but he was slow and tired. He fought well, but after fifteen long rounds Frazier won.

But Ali didn't stop fighting. After thirteen fights and twelve wins, he fought Joe Frazier again in New York in 1974. Frazier fought well, but after a long and difficult fight, this time Ali was the winner.

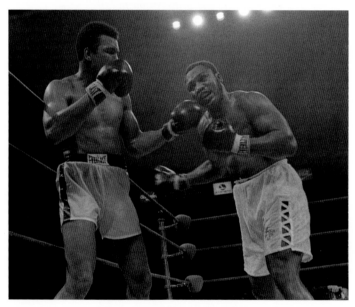

This time, Ali was the winner.

But Ali wasn't the world champion after that fight. At that time there was a new world champion, George Foreman. "I want to be world champion again," Ali said. "And only George Foreman can stop me now. When and where can I fight him?"

Ali and Foreman—The Big Fight

The Ali–Foreman fight wasn't in the U.S. It was in Kinshasa, in Zaire.* Ali loved Africa. Zaire was a black country. The government was black. Ali stayed in a beautiful big hotel, and the people there loved him.

He was on the streets of Kinshasa every day, and people called to him, "'Ali! *Bomaye!* Ali! *Bomaye!*'"

"*Bomaye?* What are they saying?" Ali asked a man.

The man had a big smile. "They're saying, "Ali! Kill him!"

Of course, George Foreman was a black American, too. But Africans loved Ali because he wanted peace in Vietnam. And he was very famous because he didn't go into the U.S. Army.

But George Foreman was a very big, strong boxer. He was twenty-five years old and Ali was thirty-two. And Foreman wasn't slow and heavy.

At four o'clock on the morning of October 30 1974, Ali and Foreman start the big fight. It is very hot in Kinshasa. There is going to be heavy rain later in the day.

In round 1 Ali starts to move and dance across the ring. Foreman comes after him. In the first round there is no winner.

*Zaire: an African country, now the Democratic Republic of Congo

Ali sits down. "I can't dance for fifteen rounds," he thinks. "It's very hot, and Foreman is quick. The old game isn't going to work."

In round 2 Ali stops dancing. He tries a new game. He is going to make his opponent tired. He moves slowly. Sometimes he only stands there. Foreman hits him with big, heavy punches. People call out, "Dance, Ali! Dance! Don't stop moving. He's killing you."

For six rounds, Foreman hits Ali again and again. But Ali stays on his feet. In round 8, Foreman is getting slow. He is very hot and tired. His hands are heavy and slow. Suddenly Ali is quick and strong again. He hits his opponent again and again. And suddenly Foreman is on the floor. He can't stand up. Ali is dancing. He is the world champion again.

He is the world champion again.

Ali stayed the champion for six years. He beat Joe Frazier again in Manila in 1975 after a long and difficult fight.

In 1978 Ali lost a fight with Leon Spinks in Las Vegas. But then, seven months later, he beat him. Ali was the new world champion three times in fourteen years.

A Quiet Time with his Family

In 1980 Ali lost a fight with Larry Holmes, and in 1981 he lost again to Trevor Burbick. He was slow and tired. He wasn't well, and he went to a doctor.

"You're very sick," the doctor said. "And you're not going to get well. It's not going to kill you, but you're going to get tired very quickly every day. You're going to walk slowly and talk slowly. I'm sorry but we can't stop it. And, of course, you can't box."

Ali stopped boxing. Now he lives quietly with his family in a big house in the country in Michigan. In the U.S. today, there are no places for "whites only." On television and in movies there are faces of all colors. People are people. Ali is happy because he was one of the first famous black Americans.

And now Ali is working for peace in the world. He makes money with his famous name. He meets and talks with governments and other famous people. He gets medals these days, too. He is a worker for peace in the world, peace for all people—blacks and whites, Christians and Muslims. In the U.S. they now say, "Ali was right. We were wrong about Vietnam. He fought for his people and for peace. He is our American Nelson Mandela."

Ali at fifty with his family.

Ali gives a lot of money to the children of the world. He loves children. He always loved children. There are nine children in his family.

He moves very slowly now. He sits at home. He gets tired very quickly. He likes watching his old fights on television. He is a good Muslim and a good man. People visit him and talk with him.

Young Muhammad Ali talked and worked for black Americans. Then he was a famous boxing champion. But today they call him a people's champion.

ACTIVITIES

Pages 1–7

Before you read

1 Look at the Word List at the back of the book. What are the words in your language?
2 Talk with two other students.
   a Name some famous boxers. Which countries do they come from?
   b What do you want to know about Muhammad Ali? Write five questions.

While you read

3 Finish the sentences.
   a Clay starts to box at .... years old.
   b The Olympic Games are in Rome in the year
      ....
   c Clay doesn't get a drink in the store in Louisville because he is ....
   d After the Olympic Games in Rome, Clay starts to box for
      ....
   e Before the fight in Miami in 1964, ... is the world champion.
   f Clay wins the fight in Miami in round ....

After you read

4 Which word is right?
   a Joe Martin is a *teacher/policeman*.
   b Clay wins an Olympic medal in *Rome/Miami*.
   c The newspapers are *right/wrong* before Clay's fight with Liston.

Pages 8–14

Before you read

5 Talk about these questions.

    a What do you know about the fighting in Vietnam (1961–75)?

    b Why did Muhammad Ali stop boxing?

    c Why do people change their name?

While you read

6 Are these sentences right (R) or wrong (W)?

    a Ali wants to go into the army and fight in Vietnam.   .....

    b In 1971 Ali fights Joe Frazier and loses.   .....

    c George Foreman doesn't hit Ali because Ali moves
very quickly.   .....

    d Ali stops boxing because he is sick.   .....

After you read

7 Answer these questions.

    a In the 1960s Ali didn't box for two years. Why not?

    b Why did the people of Zaire love Ali, and why was Ali
happy there?

    c What is Ali doing now?

Writing

8 You are Joe Martin. Cassius comes to your gym every day
and he is learning quickly. Write a letter to a friend about the
boy. Why did he first come to the gym? What is he doing
now? Is he going to be a good boxer?

9 You write for a newspaper. Clay won the fight with Liston
today. Write about the fight.

10 You are Muhammad Ali. Write a letter to your mother and
father about your time in Kinshasa.

11 Write answers to your questions from Activity 2b.

Answers for the Activities in this book are available from the Pearson English Readers
website. A free Activity Worksheet is also available from the website. Activity worksheets
are part of the Pearson English Readers Teacher Support Programme, which also
includes Progress tests and Graded Reader Guidelines. For more information,
please visit: www.pearsonenglishreaders.com